The Sermon on the Mount

A Radical Way of Being God's People

GLADYS HUNT

FISHERMAN
BIBLE STUDY SERIES

THE SERMON ON THE MOUNT

All Scripture quotations, unless otherwise indicated, are taken from the *Holy Bible, New International Version*®. NIV®. Copyright © 1973, 1978, 1984 by International Bible Society. Used by permission of Zondervan Publishing House. All rights reserved. Scripture quotations marked (KJV) are taken from the *King James Version*.

Quotations from *Studies in the Sermon on the Mount* by D. Martyn Lloyd-Jones are used by permission of Eerdmans Publishing, Grand Rapids, Michigan.

Trade Paperback ISBN 978-0-87788-316-6
eBook ISBN 978-0-307-75935-1

Published in the United States by WaterBrook, an imprint of the Crown Publishing Group, a division of Penguin Random House LLC, New York.

Printed in the United States of America
2018

35 34 33

Contents

How to Use This Studyguide

Fisherman studyguides are based on the inductive approach to Bible study. Inductive study is discovery study; we discover what the Bible says as we ask questions about its content and search for answers. This is quite different from the process in which a teacher *tells* a group *about* the Bible—what it means and what to do about it. In inductive study, God speaks directly to each of us through his Word.

A group functions best when a leader keeps the discussion on target, but the leader is neither the teacher nor the "answer person." A leader's responsibility is to *ask*—not *tell*. The answers come from the text itself as group members examine, discuss, and think together about the passage.

There are four kinds of questions in each study. The first is an *approach question*. Asked and answered before the Bible passage is read, this question breaks the ice and helps you start thinking about the topic of the Bible study. It begins to reveal where thoughts and feelings need to be transformed by Scripture.

Some of the earlier questions in each study are *observation questions*—who, what, where, when, and how—designed to help you learn some basic facts about the passage of Scripture.

Once you know what the Bible says, you need to ask, *What does it mean?* These *interpretation questions* help you discover the writer's basic message.

Next come *application questions,* which ask, *What does it mean to me?* They challenge you to live out the Scripture's life-transforming message.

Fisherman studyguides provide spaces between questions for jotting down responses as well as any related questions you would like to raise in the group. Each group member should have a copy of the studyguide and may take a turn in leading the group.

A group should use any accurate, modern translation of the Bible such as the *New International Version,* the *New American Standard Bible,* the *New Living Translation,* the *New Revised Standard Version,* the *New Jerusalem Bible,* or the *Good News Bible.* (Other translations or paraphrases of the Bible may be referred to when additional help is needed.) Bible commentaries should not be brought to a Bible study because they tend to dampen discussion and keep people from thinking for themselves.

Suggestions for Group Leaders

1. Thoroughly read and study the Bible passage before the meeting. Get a firm grasp on its themes and begin applying its teachings for yourself. Pray that the Holy Spirit will "guide you into all truth" (John 16:13) so that your leadership will guide others.

2. If any of the studyguide's questions seem ambiguous or unnatural to you, rephrase them, feeling free to add others that seem necessary to bring out the meaning of a verse.

3. Begin (and end) the study promptly. Start by asking someone to pray that every participant will both understand the passage and be open to its transforming power. Remember, the Holy Spirit is the teacher, not you!

4. Ask for volunteers to read the passages aloud.

5. As you ask the studyguide's questions in sequence, encourage everyone to participate in the discussion. If some are silent, try gently suggesting, "Let's have an answer from someone who hasn't spoken up yet."

6. If a question comes up that you can't answer, don't be afraid to admit that you're baffled. Assign the topic as a research project for someone to report on next week, or say, "I'll do some studying and let you know what I find out."

7. Keep the discussion moving, but be sure it stays focused. Though a certain number of tangents are inevitable, you'll want to quickly bring the discussion back to the topic at hand. Also, learn to pace the discussion so that you finish the lesson in the time allotted.

8. Don't be afraid of silences; some questions take time to answer, and some people need time to gather courage to speak. If silence persists, rephrase your question, but resist the temptation to answer it yourself.

9. If someone comes up with an answer that is clearly illogical or unbiblical, ask for further clarification: "What verse suggests that to you?"

10. Discourage overuse of cross references. Learn all you can from the passage at hand, while selectively incorporating a few important references suggested in the studyguide.

11. Some questions are marked with a ⊘. This indicates that further information is available in the Leader's Notes at the back of the guide.

12. For more information on getting a new Bible study group started and keeping it functioning effectively, read *You Can Start a Bible Study Group* by Gladys M. Hunt and *Pilgrims in Progress: Growing Through Groups* by Jim and Carol Plueddemann. (Both books are available from Shaw Books.)

SUGGESTIONS FOR GROUP MEMBERS

1. Learn and apply the following ground rules for effective Bible study. (If new members join the group later, review these guidelines with the whole group.)

2. Remember that your goal is to learn all you can *from the Bible passage being studied.* Let it speak for itself without using Bible commentaries or other Bible passages. There is more than enough in each assigned passage to keep your group productively occupied for one session. Sticking to the passage saves the group from insecurity ("I don't have the right reference books—or the time to read anything else.") and confusion ("Where did *that* come from? I thought we were studying _____.").

3. Avoid the temptation to bring up those fascinating tangents that don't really grow out of the passage you are discussing. If the topic is of common interest, you can bring it up later in informal conversation after the study. Meanwhile, help one another stick to the subject.

4. Encourage one another to participate. People remember best what they discover and verbalize for

themselves. Some people are naturally shy, while others may be afraid of making a mistake. If your discussion is free and friendly and you show real interest in what other group members think and feel, the quieter ones will be more likely to speak up. Remember, the more people involved in a discussion, the richer it will be.

5. Guard yourself from answering too many questions or talking too much. Give others a chance to share their ideas. If you are one who participates easily, discipline yourself by counting to ten before you open your mouth.

6. Make personal, honest applications and commit yourself to letting God's Word change you.

Introduction

Perhaps there is no more tragic comment in Scripture than the one in John 1:10-11: "He [Jesus] was in the world, and though the world was made through him, the world did not recognize him. He came to that which was his own, but his own did not receive him."

The Jews were looking for someone who would restore their political fortunes to the glory they had known in the days of King David. They hoped that the coming Messiah would bring emancipation from the rule of Rome. The kingdom of God, in their minds, was an external, political one involving military and material success. That is why so many did not recognize and often could not hear the words of Jesus Christ.

Although the Sermon on the Mount is very familiar to many of us, it would have been startling to an audience in Palestine in the days of Jesus. He told of a kingdom that had in fact *already come*. He spoke of a kingdom that "is at hand" as well as a kingdom that "will come." But strangest of all, he said that "the kingdom is within you." The kingdom is *the life of God in us*. If we study the Sermon on the Mount carefully, we discover that it is all an elaboration of what it means to love God with our hearts and minds and to love our neighbor as ourselves.

Why should we study this highly quotable but puzzling section of the New Testament? First, because the God who gives us these teachings is the God who understands us completely. Jesus does not tell us, "Live like this and you will become Christians," but rather, "Because you are Christians, live like this." It is his instruction handbook especially for us who believe in him. The Lord Jesus Christ died to enable us to live out these principles (see Titus 2:14).

Second, the Sermon on the Mount shows us our great need of a Savior. When these teachings of Jesus pierce our hearts, we see our utter helplessness and our great need for spiritual birth. Only the Holy Spirit, the life of God in us, can make it possible for us to live this way. The Sermon on the Mount drives us to the Savior.

And, third, living out this sermon will mean blessing in our lives. "Blessed are you when…" In our contemporary experience-oriented and emotion-oriented culture, we need to look again at what brings genuine joy. "Blessed are those who hunger and thirst for righteousness, for they will be filled."

The Sermon on the Mount encapsulates teaching from both the Old and New Testaments. When you read the apostle Paul's writings, for example, you will find repeated emphasis on these instructions from Jesus's longest recorded sermon. The world's values are turned upside down in this call to radical discipleship.

The Christian's Character—Part I

MATTHEW 5:1-6

ave you ever met anyone whose claim to be acceptably "religious" is that he or she "just lives by the Sermon on the Mount"? Maybe you've said those words yourself without studying the profound implications of Jesus's teachings. His idea of "happy" or "blessed" doesn't start where ours does.

In this well-known passage of Scripture called the Beatitudes, Jesus did not tell us what to do in order to gain happiness. Rather, he described the character of a person who *is* happy or blessed.

1. Suppose you are eager to join an organization (maybe a fraternity, a club, or a sports team). Would you expect admittance based on your good points or your weaknesses? Explain.

READ MATTHEW 5:1-6.

2. Why must a person acknowledge spiritual need in order to enter the kingdom of heaven?

    What makes it difficult for people to believe that God accepts them on those terms?

✎3. What does it mean to be poor in spirit?

4. How does the emphasis in verse 3 differ from the emphasis our culture places on self?

5. What is our natural reaction to mourning? Why?

---

6. By declaring mourners as "blessed," what part of life was Jesus affirming?

7. What kinds of mourning are there?

   How can mourning fit in with poverty of spirit?

   What kind of comfort do such mourners receive?

8. Contrast what Jesus said in verse 5 with the general human concepts of power and meekness.

9. What does meekness *not* mean?

10. How does meekness work out in everyday life?

11. What promise is given to the meek?

Do you see this happening in any way? Explain.

12. Put verse 6 into your own words.

What characterizes a person who hungers and thirsts?

What is this "righteousness"?

13. Describe a person you know who hungers and thirsts after righteousness. What freedoms does such a person have?

14. How does your own personal hunger for righteousness affect your sense of fulfillment in life?

The Christian's Character—Part 2

MATTHEW 5:7-12

The non-Christian world often has a good idea of what humanity needs. We hear that the world needs peace, for instance. But the human ways of seeking peace are seldom the ways of God. In fact, without God's Spirit operating in us, we tend to use destructive means to establish good results. Thus, the person of Christian character is forever at odds with the world. It is not surprising that Jesus ended the Beatitudes with words on persecution.

1. In what ways have you seen your value system opposed by the world's system?

READ MATHEW 5:7-9.

2. What does it mean to be merciful?

How does mercy go beyond feeling mere pity for another person?

How does being merciful relate to truth? (Does a merciful person ignore wrongdoing?)

3. How does experiencing mercy affect a person's ability to be merciful to others? Can you give an example of this from your own life?

4. What promise is given to the merciful?

From whom do they receive mercy?

5. What does it mean to be pure in heart (verse 8)? Give several synonyms that help clarify the meaning.

What is the difference between purity and innocence? What is our part in purity?

6. In what ways do you think the pure in heart see God?

7. What hope do the pure in heart have for the future?

How can this hope affect life today?

8. How would verse 9 have sounded to the Jews who were hoping Jesus would bring liberation from Roman rule?

9. What are the characteristics of a peacemaker?

10. What is the difference between a peacemaker and an appeaser? In what ways is peace more than absence of conflict?

Why are peacemakers called the children of God?

READ MATTHEW 5:10-12.

11. How does persecution fit in with the Beatitudes listed in Matthew 5:3-9? (For instance, why would a peacemaker be persecuted?)

12. What is the reason for the persecution mentioned in verse 11?

What is the difference between *being offensive* and *causing offense because we are righteous?*

13. For what reasons is this kind of persecution cause for rejoicing?

Are you willing to live in opposition to popular opinion? In what areas of life is this most difficult for you?

14. What can you learn about Christian growth from the progression of the Beatitudes?

The Christian in the World

MATTHEW 5:13-16

One of the most famous phrases in any speech by former president George Bush Sr. is "a thousand points of light." People ever since have used those words to describe individuals, organizations, or events that make a positive difference in the world.

Two thousand years ago, Jesus said to a crowd not quite so large or sophisticated, "You are the light of the world." He also said, "You are the salt of the earth." "Salt of the earth" in American culture refers to people who are good, genuine, and dependable. As we look at Jesus's original teaching, we find stronger and more radical meanings of salt and light.

1. What are some ways in which Christians have made a positive difference in the world?

READ MATTHEW 5:13.

2. For centuries, and in Jesus's time, salt was used not only to flavor food but also to preserve it. What does this need for salt imply about the world?

✗3. Why must a Christian be like salt?

What is significant about the presence or absence of salt?

4. How does the individual Christian function as salt? Give some practical illustrations of this.

How does the body of Christ—the church—function as salt? Give examples.

5. What is the worth of saltless salt? How might a Christian lose his or her "saltiness"?

READ MATTHEW 5:14-16.

6. What is the function of light? What two illustrations did Jesus use to explain our being light?

7. Where does the world look for its light? What evidence is there that technology and increased knowledge and information have not brought the light that people have hoped for?

8. What can disciples do to become the light the world needs?

How are we sometimes tempted to hide our light?

9. How does the world react to light? Look at the following passage from John:

> This is the verdict: Light has come into the world,
> but men loved darkness instead of light because their
> deeds were evil. Everyone who does evil hates the
> light, and will not come into the light for fear that
> his deeds will be exposed. But whoever lives by the
> truth comes into the light, so that it may be seen
> plainly that what he has done has been done through
> God. (John 3:19-21)

How does light expose the cause of darkness?

10. What do salt and light have in common? What conclusions can we make about ourselves if we claim to be Christians and yet are reluctant to be salt and light?

11. What should be the result of letting our light shine?

12. In what ways are you functioning as salt and light?

    Is there a bowl you must remove in your life to let your light shine? Be specific.

The Christian and God's Law

MATTHEW 5:17-20

I t's hard for us to imagine how important the Law was in the Jewish world. It governed everything a good Jew did from early morning until night. The job of the "lawyers" of Israel (the scribes and Pharisees) was to protect the Law and explain it. The true purpose of the Law got scrambled as they labored over its interpretation, tightening up what wasn't important and making loopholes for what was.

The scribes saw Jesus and his teaching as a disruption to their work. They considered him unorthodox. Yet Jesus in this sermon made it clear that he had come to defend and fulfill the true meaning of the Law. He went beyond the words of the Law to the inner spirit of the person.

1. Name one or two laws—such as those having to do with traffic, possessions, or relationships—and

briefly discuss what principles those rules represent and protect.

READ MATTHEW 5:17-20.

2. Why did Jesus say he had come?

To what does "the Law or the Prophets" refer (verse 17)?

3. Why might some people have thought Jesus had come to abolish the Law?

In what ways do Christians today sometimes convey such an attitude toward the Old Testament?

✐ 4. How did Jesus emphasize the Law's importance in verses 17 and 18?

What encouragement can such statements give to Christians about Scripture?

5. How does our response to the Law affect our standing in God's kingdom?

In what ways can we teach others to keep God's commands?

✐ 6. How carefully did the scribes and Pharisees keep the Law? What was wrong with their spiritual lives?

7. How can we personally apply the warnings of verse 20?

   What is the "righteousness" our Lord expects of his disciples?

8. A quick look at the books of the Law (Genesis through Deuteronomy) reveals a system of ethics that ordered a peaceful, productive society; respected and worshiped God; and honored the worth of others. From what you know of Jesus, in what ways was his life a fulfillment of the Law?

9. The prophets constantly called people to leave their idols, worship God, and love their neighbors. How is the Christian message a fulfillment of the prophets' message?

10. In what ways has this study influenced your thinking on the value of the Old Testament?

11. How can your righteousness exceed that of the scribes and Pharisees?

STUDY 5

The Christian's Understanding of Sin

MATTHEW 5:21-30

One of the first words a baby understands is *no*. From our toddling years on, we maintain a growing catalog of things we are *not* to do. Along with this moral system comes the sense that as long as we refrain from certain negative or sinful activities, we will be good people.

Sin goes much deeper than actions, and a spiritually discerning Christian grows in awareness of its subtle traps.

1. Describe the first time (or one of the first times) you recognized how deeply sin was ingrained in your thoughts, motives, and emotions.

READ MATTHEW 5:21-30.

2. What pattern do you observe in the series of statements Jesus made in this passage (verses 21-22, 27-28)?

3. What one basic principle was Jesus laying down in each of his illustrations?

What can we do to apply this principle to all of life to help us define true holiness?

4. Give a contemporary example of obeying the meaning of the Law, not just the technicality.

5. As Jesus explained the commandment, what attitudes and actions did he include in "Do not murder"?

6. Does this mean a Christian should never be angry? Define the inner attitude of the anger Jesus was speaking about in verse 22.

7. What is the main point of verses 23-26?

   Why is it important to settle conflicts quickly?

8. Based on verses 27-30, how would you define what sin really is?

How seriously did Jesus view the destructive nature of sin (verses 29-30)? Explain.

9. How does Jesus's expansion of the commandment in verse 27 reflect the character of the God who gave it to us?

10. Note what vital, essential parts of the body Jesus used in his dramatic illustrations. What principle for a holy life did he give us in these verses?

11. Give a practical example of how verses 29 and 30 might be put into action in daily life.

STUDY 6

The Christian's Integrity

MATTHEW 5:31-37

Jesus was familiar with our ability to rationalize our actions as well as our ability to make up for lack of substance with an excess of words. To get the attention of his hearers on these matters, he pushed two "hot buttons" of the day: divorce and oath taking.

1. Describe a time when you rationalized actions because, technically, there was nothing wrong with them.

READ MATTHEW 5:31-32.

2. Looking at this passage, what was Jesus's view of the permanence of marriage? the concession of divorce?

3. Why is adultery so serious a matter in God's sight?

READ MATTHEW 5:33-37.

4. What was the purpose behind the particular law described in verse 33? Why do you think it was necessary?

5. Why do people take oaths or make vows? What is the danger of such an action, especially if God's name is used?

6. What did Jesus teach about oath taking in verses 34-37? What kinds of oaths do people use today?

7. Does this mean one should never take an oath in a court of law? Why or why not? (Quakers interpret this passage this way.)

8. If the Spirit of Truth dwells in us, what will happen to our white lies and exaggerations? How does he enable us to let our yes be yes and our no be no?

9. In what ways would ordinary truthfulness and simple integrity in keeping promises change business, community, marriage, family, and even world relationships?

10. In what area of life are you challenged to have more integrity?

The Christian's Treatment of Others

MATTHEW 5:38-48

Most people have a reasonably good sense of fairness. They seem to know intuitively whether an incident or remark is just or unjust. Many editorials, letters, and books have been written, many speeches made, and many public demonstrations staged, all in the name of doing "what's fair."

Jesus knocked those well-ingrained ideas off balance when he approached this subject. Enter: mercy and aggressive love.

1. When have you felt satisfied about getting what you deserved? When has such justice not been a positive experience?

Read Matthew 5:38-42.

✐2. How would the Mosaic legislation of verse 38 take care of the excesses of revenge?

Does this law require that there must always be an eye for an eye? If not, what do you think was the spirit of the original law?

3. What contemporary examples of the situations in verses 39-41 can you think of?

4. What makes it difficult to live out the approach Jesus described in verses 39-42?

5. What personal rights seem to be violated by verses 39-42? How would living out verses 41 and 42 show a different quality of life to the world?

6. What does this principle teach us about how we should view possessions?

READ MATTHEW 5:43-48.

7. How had the Pharisees taught the law regarding love to others?

8. What is to be the Christian's attitude toward others?

9. How does God expect us to reflect the spiritual life he has given us in Christ?

10. How is relationship emphasized in verses 45 and 48?

11. Look again at verses 46 and 47. How does this attitude manifest itself in us today? Give some examples.

12. How would you sum up the teaching of this lesson's passage?

What can you do to apply any part of it to your situation?

The Christian's Religion

MATTHEW 6:1-8,16-18

F ew people want to be labeled *religious*. Ask a person why this is so, and the answer will surely confirm the teaching of this study. *Religion* has come to mean status quo, aiming to impress, self-righteousness, and competition for the most "holy" reputation. Quite often *religious* is synonymous with *hypocritical*.

Jesus wanted to set the record straight. And what he revealed about the truly religious life would both liberate and enrich those ready to apply his teachings.

1. Think of a truly religious person you respect. What is distinctive about him or her?

READ MATTHEW 6:1-8, 16-18.

✐ 2. Scan these passages and note the references to God. What name is he given? How many times did Jesus refer to him?

What do we learn about the Father?

3. What motive was Jesus warning against?

4. What areas of personal religious life are covered in this passage?

5. Reward is involved in each of these areas. Contrast the kinds of rewards given.

6. What does it mean to not "let your left hand know what your right hand is doing"? Who keeps the accounts?

   How can we become less self-conscious about the worthy things we do?

7. What principles for your prayer life do you find in verses 5-8?

What do you understand from the instruction to "close the door" (verse 6)?

8. If, as stated in verse 8, our Father knows what we need before we ask him, why should we pray?

9. What is the purpose of fasting?

10. Contrast the right and wrong way to fast.

What should be our focus when we fast?

11. How do these verses point to our constant need to deal with our self-centeredness in the Christian life?

12. How would you evaluate your prayer life in light of the standards given in this study? How would you evaluate the help you give others? What steps can you take to grow in these areas?

The Christian's Prayer

MATTHEW 6:9-15

More energy is likely expended in churches learning about prayer than actually praying. But people have always wanted to know how to approach a holy God. A parallel passage to today's text is Luke 11:1-4, in which the disciples came to Jesus and said, "Lord, teach us to pray."

Jesus's model prayer is quite simple, but its principles provide much to meditate on. They help us understand what prayer really is. How fortunate we are that Jesus gave us the key to communion with himself.

1. Briefly discuss a phrase from the Lord's Prayer that has always intrigued you.

READ MATTHEW 6:9-15.

✐ 2.   How did Jesus address God as he began this model
prayer?

Notice Jesus said *our* Father, and in so doing, he
linked the disciples to himself in a family relationship. What confidence does this give you at the very
outset of learning to pray?

3.   Why do you think Jesus used the phrase "Our
Father in heaven" (verse 9)? What does this descrip-
tive phrase tell you about the Father?

✐ 4.   What three petitions follow that relate to God's
glory? Notice that each phrase contains *your*.

5. What do we mean when we pray, "Hallowed be your name" (verse 9)?

6. Why do we need to pray, "Your kingdom come" (verse 10)?

Exactly what are you praying for when you pray this phrase in the Lord's Prayer?

7. What areas do the next three petitions in verses 11-13 cover?

In what ways do these petitions cover what we need in life?

8. With a freezer full of food, enough to last for weeks, how can you pray for daily bread and really mean it? In what way are you utterly dependent upon God for your daily bread?

In what ways does a daily consciousness of this dependence affect your Christian life and your attitude toward God? In what ways does it affect the act of giving thanks at meals?

9. With verses 14 and 15 in mind, what does it mean to pray, "Forgive us our debts, as we also have forgiven our debtors" (verse 12)? Is this a legal forgiving that we receive *because* we have forgiven our debtors? If not, why not?

What effect does the knowledge of personal forgiveness have on a person? Why is this one of our basic needs?

10. What is the deliverance we are to pray for? On what basis do we have the right to pray this petition?

11. Review the Lord's Prayer in its entirety. In what order do the requests appear? What practical principles does this give you for your own prayer life? In particular, what do you learn about coming into God's presence?

The Christian's Treasure

MATTHEW 6:19-34

Although Jesus did draw the attention of people from every social strata, he preached mostly to "common folk." Many who followed him had been debilitated by disease or demon possession; consequently, they would have been among the poorest in Palestine. So it seems strange that Jesus would warn them about storing up treasure. Or does it?

Jesus understood the human tendency to possess, hoard, and measure worth by material status, whether one is rich or poor. What he really talked about in this passage is *how we are fulfilled.*

1. Under what circumstances are you the most concerned about money and material goods?

Read Matthew 6:19-24.

2. What did Jesus mean by *treasure?* How does one store up treasure on earth?

How does this warning apply to poor people? to rich people?

3. In what ways are we often ensnared by treasure?

Can treasure sometimes have a spiritual appearance? Explain.

4. What positive instruction did the Lord give about treasure? How does one store up treasure in heaven?

5. Contrast the security of heavenly treasure with that of earthly treasure. Who guards the heavenly treasure?

In what ways is earthly treasure of any kind constantly endangered?

6. How can we tell where our treasure really is? List some practical indicators that will help us see what our values are (e.g., how do we spend our time?).

7. How did Jesus use the illustration of the eye to teach us about our value systems?

8. How have you seen verse 24 demonstrated in contemporary life?

Discuss why true Christianity and materialism cannot be compatible.

READ MATTHEW 6:25-34.

9. Repetition is a good teaching tool. What instruction did Jesus repeatedly give?

10. What does it mean to worry?

    What are we not to worry about? How does this relate to storing up treasure on earth (Matthew 6:19)?

11. Some people believe that everything in life is accidental, that there is no real order or purpose to life. Others believe that "what will be will be," that events are somehow determined by fate, which is

out of our control. In what ways is the Christian view of life, which Jesus spoke about in this study, different from either of these?

12. In what ways do we unconsciously reveal whether we believe God to be sufficient for the whole of our lives? Be specific.

13. Where is your treasure? Have you chosen God or material things? Discuss.

The Christian's Discernment

MATTHEW 7:1-6

When it comes to making judgments, it seems there is no safe ground. On the one hand, people who articulate strong opinions—particularly opinions that are accepted in society—are thought to be wise, witty, even on the cutting edge. Yet if a person meekly speaks against activities that God has pronounced sinful, he or she will likely be labeled a fanatic, a do-gooder, or, worst of all, judgmental.

How is a Christian to relate with discernment and true holiness to a world that is basically opposed to God's value system? Jesus gave us some very basic but potent principles.

1. Think of a person who seems to you to be judgmental. Why does that adjective, rather than the words *discerning* or *wise*, come to mind?

READ MATTHEW 7:1-6.

2. Why are we to be careful about the judgments we make?

How will our own judgments affect us?

3. What is the inner attitude against which Jesus warned?

4. Give an example of "specks of sawdust" and "planks."

5. What evidence is there in these verses that we *should* make judgments?

On what basis does a person become capable of making such judgments?

6. How is verse 1 often taken out of context? Give specific examples.

7. What is the difference between *judgment* and *discernment,* as we commonly understand these words?

8. What specific discernment is needed to obey verse 6?

What kind of people do you think Jesus was describing here?

9. What happens when something holy and valuable is given to the wrong people?

Put the meaning of verse 6 in contemporary language.

10. How does this teaching about judging fit in with the whole of the Sermon on the Mount?

11. Ask yourself the following questions:

In what areas must I stop judging others?

In what areas must I sharpen my judgments?

Write out your personal prayer as you ask for God's help with personal discernment and honesty.

The Christian's Expectation

MATTHEW 7:7-12

A typical revival-time question has always been, "Are you willing for God to do with you whatever he pleases?" A question that is *not* so typical is, "Are you willing for God to give you all the gifts he's prepared for you?" Yet a balanced view of Scripture reveals a God who longs to give many good things to his children.

Jesus understood that people feared God more than they loved God. He had to use some exaggerated examples to help us see that God is waiting to hear not only our praise but also our requests.

1. What are your wildest dreams in life? Would you consider handing this wish list to God? Why or why not?

READ MATTHEW 7:7-12.

2. List the active verbs in verse 7. How would you
   describe the intensity of these verbs?

   What is the result of such persistence?

3. Does this verse mean that you can ask for *anything*,
   and God will give it to you?

   Would you want that kind of arrangement? Why or
   why not?

4. In light of all we've studied so far, what are we to ask
   for and to seek?

5. In view of the promise in verses 7 and 8, why is the quality of our Christian living so poor?

Why are we changeable and inconsistent in persistently seeking spiritual good? Give some personal examples of spiritual resolutions you have made that have fallen by the wayside.

6. How is persistence an amplification of the fourth beatitude: "Blessed are those who hunger and thirst for righteousness, for they will be filled"?

7. What comparison did Jesus make in these verses to assure us that we will receive what we ask?

How would the constant realization that God is your Father change your daily life? Be specific.

8. What contrasts did Jesus make between our earthly fathers and our heavenly Father? What word describes the gifts our heavenly Father gives?

9. Look back through Matthew 5 and review every statement Jesus made about the Law and the Prophets. How does the teaching in Matthew 7:12 fit in with what Jesus previously taught?

10. What would happen if the Golden Rule were practiced instead of merely admired (verse 12)? How would your family life change?

Why is this such a difficult rule to follow? Discuss ways to sharpen your awareness of the spirit of this rule.

11. In most translations, verse 12 begins with *therefore* or *so,* giving it a strong connective link with the teaching of the preceding verses. According to verses 9-11, does God give us what we deserve? How does he deal with us? How does verse 12 fit into this context?

12. Ask yourself these questions:

Why are my prayers often unanswered?

What do I most want from God as I ask, seek, and knock?

On what basis do I know that God answers prayer?

The Christian's Direction

MATTHEW 7:13-20

This is the age of options. We can choose many fields of study and work. We can live in any number of places. We can choose from scores of churches in a single city, from scores of different cuisines in a single restaurant district. What used to be "Coffee or tea?" is now "Coffee—regular or decaf; tea—regular, decaf, or herbal; or soda—decaf, sugar-free, or classic?"

We love our power to choose, making minute distinctions between fields of vocational expertise or combinations of herbs in our main dish. But when it comes to life's most important decisions, we'd rather not get pinned down—which is exactly what Jesus does to us in this pointed lesson.

1. What decisions are hardest for you? Why?

READ MATTHEW 7:13-14.

2. What decision are we asked to make?

Why is this decision not an easy one to make?

3. Compare the two gates (or the two ways of life) in these verses.

Which way do we naturally follow, and why? Why do we find it hard to limit our options?

4. What teaching in these verses seems hard or narrow to you as compared with the world's thinking? Explain.

What is left behind when a person chooses to enter at the narrow gate? Which gate requires us to focus our life?

READ MATTHEW 7:15-20.

    𝒪 5. Of what danger did Jesus warn his followers? Why are false prophets so dangerous?

    6. Discuss what kind of person a false prophet might be in today's culture.

        How might false prophets dissuade a disciple from entering the narrow gate? What teachings might they avoid?

    7. How are we to recognize false prophets? What illustration did Jesus use to drive home his point?

8. How did Jesus re-emphasize that being a Christian affects the very center of a person's being?

What is the fruit that tests our lives?

9. What warnings do you find in Matthew 7:13-20? What encouragements?

10. What can you do to remain on the narrow road from day to day?

11. What discernment is required to obey Jesus's instructions?

The Christian's Response

MATTHEW 7:21-29

I t is rare to find a person who doesn't want to learn. Whether in technological, scholastic, artistic, or spiritual areas, we clamor for more knowledge. It must have been much the same in Jesus's time; we see him followed by crowds and quizzed by the most knowledgeable people of the day.

But Jesus recognized a fatal flaw in people. It takes more than knowledge to please God and live out a kingdom lifestyle. Consequently, the famous Sermon on the Mount ends with a not-so-famous warning.

1. Make a list of the learning activities that have taken place in your spiritual journey. Include revivals, seminars, classes, workshops, and retreats. Discuss the changes some of these brought about in your life.

Read Matthew 7:21-29.

2. What can be said of the orthodoxy and zeal of the people about whom Jesus spoke in verses 21 and 22?

In what ways can belief be superficial even though it may be intensely active?

3. According to verse 22, why is it easy to be fooled by these false Christians?

4. Contrast the declaration of the false prophets with Jesus's declaration.

5. What did the two men in verses 24-27 have in common?

In what ways do we hear Jesus's words today?

6. What is the only difference between the two houses mentioned here? When does this difference become obvious?

7. What are the characteristics of a spiritually foolish person? Give examples.

8. What are the characteristics of a spiritually wise person? Give examples.

9. What are the important characteristics of the rock mentioned in verse 24? Apply the principle of an adequate foundation to your own life.

10. At the conclusion of Jesus's sermon, how did the audience react (verses 28-29)?

What did they recognize about Jesus?

11. Ask yourself these questions to conclude this study:

What is the basic foundation on which I am building my life?

In what specific areas do I find obedience difficult? (Take time to pray, giving these areas to God and asking for his help.)

What specific things do I want to change in my life as a result of studying the Sermon on the Mount?

Leader's Notes

STUDY 1: THE CHRISTIAN'S CHARACTER—PART 1

Question 3. "In Matthew, Jesus pronounces 'the poor in spirit' blessed. In Luke 6:20, it is simply 'the poor.'... In the Greco-Roman world, the 'poor' simply applied to those who lived in material poverty. In the Old Testament, however, the term 'poor'...[referred to] the humble pious who were beloved by God (Isaiah 61:1).... [A]n empty purse did not allow the needy to be pushy or haughty. The poor had no material resources, no security.... Those who were helpless and who knew they were helpless could not rely on their financial muscle but had to wait on God.... With this background, we can see that Matthew's version, 'poor in spirit', is basically identical to Luke's 'poor.'... 'The poor in spirit' are those who live in humble acknowledgment of their impoverishment before God.... The poor in spirit are those who humbly recognize their dependence on God" (David S. Dockery and David E. Garland, *Seeking the Kingdom: The Sermon on the Mount Made Practical for Today,* Wheaton, IL: Harold Shaw Publishers, 1992, pp. 19-20).

Question 9. "In the ancient world, meekness connoted power that was bridled by gentleness. That is why the ancient Greeks did not say 'meek as a mouse' but 'meek as a lion.' It referred to controlled strength.

"Moses is described as meek when he did not repay the slander of Miriam and Aaron but beseeched the Lord to cure

Miriam from her leprosy (Numbers 12:3-13). Jesus describes himself as being 'meek and lowly' (Matthew 11:29, KJV)" (Dockery and Garland, *Seeking the Kingdom,* p. 24).

Question 13. Much human energy is spent seeking happiness. This verse tells us to hunger and thirst not after happiness but after righteousness. Nor are we to hanker after experiences, even if they are religious ones. Happiness, or blessedness, is the result of a hunger for righteousness.

STUDY 2: THE CHRISTIAN'S CHARACTER—PART 2

Question 5. "To be pure in heart may refer either to sinlessness of the heart or to singleness of heart. According to the first view, Jesus is alluding to inner purity. Those who are pure in heart have pure thoughts (Matthew 5:28) and pure motives (Matthew 6:1-6,16-18).... According to the second view, Jesus has in mind the person with a one-track mind when it comes to the things of God. The pure in heart are those who center their lives wholly upon God (see Matthew 22:37). For example, James tells his readers: 'Come near to God and he will come near to you. Wash your hands, you sinners, and purify your hearts, you double-minded' (James 4:8)" (Dockery and Garland, *Seeking the Kingdom,* pp. 29-30).

We are definitely responsible up to a point for our own holiness. Note these verses:

> Put to death, therefore, whatever belongs to your earthly
> nature: sexual immorality, impurity, lust, evil desires and
> greed, which is idolatry. (Colossians 3:5)

Therefore, as God's chosen people, holy and dearly loved, clothe yourselves with compassion, kindness, humility, gentleness and patience. Bear with each other and forgive whatever grievances you may have against one another. Forgive as the Lord forgave you. (Colossians 3:12-13)

Come near to God and he will come near to you. Wash your hands, you sinners, and purify your hearts, you double-minded. Grieve, mourn and wail. Change your laughter to mourning and your joy to gloom. Humble yourselves before the Lord, and he will lift you up. (James 4:8-10)

Question 10. Notice how God himself is described (in relation to peace) in the following verses: John 14:27; 16:33; Romans 5:1; 15:33; Ephesians 2:14-16; Philippians 4:9; Hebrews 13:20.

Question 14. The Beatitudes are not a collection of random ideas; they build on each other. The kingdom of heaven is for those who realize their spiritual poverty—they mourn over their sins, they are sensitive to their master, they hunger and thirst for righteousness, and so on.

STUDY 3: THE CHRISTIAN IN THE WORLD

Question 3. "The very characteristic of saltiness proclaims a difference, for a small amount of salt in a large medium is at once apparent. Unless we are clear about this we have not even begun to think correctly about the Christian life. The Christian is a person who is essentially different from everybody else.

He is as different as salt is from the meat into which it is rubbed. He is as different as the salt is from the wound into which it is put" (D. Martyn Lloyd-Jones, *Studies in the Sermon on the Mount,* Grand Rapids: Eerdmans, 1971, p. 153).

Question 8. Ephesians 5:1-21 is a helpful, practical passage for understanding the meaning of being light in a dark world.

STUDY 4: THE CHRISTIAN AND GOD'S LAW

Question 2. Whenever the expression "the Law and the Prophets" is used in the New Testament, it refers to the Old Testament Scriptures. To a Jew, the Pentateuch (the first five books of the Old Testament) was "the Law." The remainder of the Old Testament Scriptures were known as "the Prophets," though they included poetic and historical books as well.

Question 4. Jesus wants us to see that holy living is a positive thing, not just a negative attitude. People want a set of rules so they can say, "If I don't do that, I am holy." Such a negative attitude insults the nature of God. Hungering and thirsting after righteousness is a positive, eager way to live. Jesus wants us to have the freedom to develop spiritual character—not just to be negative keepers of the letter of the Law. We might well ask ourselves, "Are the Ten Commandments repressive, enslaving laws, or are they God's outline for freedom and healthy relationships?"

Question 6. During his Sermon on the Mount, Jesus did not elaborate on the lifestyles of the religious leaders he named; however, some knowledge of their spirituality is important to understanding this point of the sermon. Over the years the scribes and Pharisees had become quite legalistic, creating scores of smaller laws from the original laws God had given the Israelites. These laws were almost impossible to keep track of and to apply, particularly for the unlearned (most of the Jewish population). Not only legalistic, these leaders were also obsessive about practicing the finer points of their laws at the expense of justice and mercy, the actual intent of God's law. They were known for taking advantage of the very people they should have been protecting—orphans, widows, the poor, and aliens. For a detailed description of Jesus's approach to the scribes and Pharisees, scan Matthew 23.

STUDY 5: THE CHRISTIAN'S UNDERSTANDING OF SIN

Question 2. "You have heard it said" refers to the law as the Pharisees had been teaching it, not to the Mosaic Law.

STUDY 6: THE CHRISTIAN'S INTEGRITY

Question 2. In Deuteronomy 24:1-4, Moses introduced a civil law to protect women who were being mistreated because of the sin of lust. This is the Mosaic ruling Jesus was referring to here. God's plan for marriage is found in Genesis 2:24. Later, the Pharisees tried to trip Jesus up on the question of divorce (Matthew 19:3-9).

Question 3. To keep the chaos of sin at a minimum, Moses permitted divorce with certain restrictions. In Matthew 19:3-9, Jesus referred back to the original plan of God, which involves *oneness:* a man and a woman becoming one flesh. Our Lord went back to the great principle that God had in mind at Creation: the indissolubility of marriage. Sin has pressured people to find ways of getting around God's plan in order to fulfill their own lusts. Again, Jesus went beyond the letter of the Law or the concessions of Mosaic civil legislation to get at the heart of what God had in mind for men and women. It involves the issue of our heart's attitude before God—the very center of our being in tune with his plan.

Question 4. The wording "You have heard that it was said" referred to a Pharisaic interpretation of the third commandment—Exodus 20:7—and its associated instructions in Leviticus 19:12 and Deuteronomy 6:13.

Question 7. Numbers 30 contains the legislation as to how and when vows should be taken, so it is difficult to conclude that God has no use for vows. Other passages in the Old Testament also speak of vows. See Psalm 61:5,8.

STUDY 7: THE CHRISTIAN'S TREATMENT OF OTHERS

Question 2. "The principle of justice must come in, and justice is never excessive in its demands. There is a correspondence between the crime and the punishment, the thing done and what is to be done about it. The object of that law was not to urge men to take an eye for an eye and a tooth for a tooth, and to insist upon it every time; it was simply meant to avoid this horrible excess, this terrible spirit of revenge and demand for restitution and to check it and hold it within bounds. But perhaps the most important thing is that this enactment was not given to the individual, but rather to the judges who were responsible for law and order among individuals" (Lloyd-Jones, *Studies in the Sermon on the Mount,* p. 272).

Question 5. The epistles of James, John, and Paul enlarge this principle and show us its balance. While John said that to refrain from giving to someone in need demonstrates an absence of love (1 John 3:17-18) and James said it indicates a lack of true faith (James 2:14-17), Paul, in a substantial passage (2 Thessalonians 3:6-15), instructed the church to be very direct in its discipline toward those believers who are idle ("If a man will not work, he shall not eat").

Question 7. Nowhere does the Old Testament say this. The Pharisees made up an interpretation in which *neighbor* meant a fellow Jew, and *enemy* meant a Gentile.

Question 8. We must not confuse *love* with *like.* God is not commanding us to feel a certain way toward people who may be quite unlikable and even hateful toward us. "But love entails that we are concerned about the welfare of another. It means that we will do things that will benefit and not harm the other" (Dockery and Garland, *Seeking the Kingdom,* p. 67).

Earthly civilizations have often proclaimed ethics that hint at this godly principle. For example, the Geneva Convention requires that prisoners of war be fed, sheltered, and given medical treatment. They remain "enemies," but that does not justify neglecting their general welfare as human beings. These rules of civility are often ignored, but nations of the world value the existence of international laws such as these; they are a symbol of basic human worth.

STUDY 8: THE CHRISTIAN'S RELIGION

Question 2. Father is a family word that Jesus introduced to those who become the children of God. It is the Christian name for God. The Jews had been so in awe of the holiness of God that they scarcely dared to say his name. Imagine what a revolutionary concept this was—to say "your Father."

Question 5. For further study on *rewards,* see Hebrews 11:8-10,13-16,24-26 and 12:1-2.

Question 9. "Fasting—going without food in order to spend time in prayer—is noble *and* difficult. It gives us time to pray, teaches self-discipline, reminds us that we can live with a lot less, and helps us appreciate God's gifts. Jesus was not condemning fasting, but hypocrisy—fasting in order to gain approval from people. Fasting was mandatory for the Jewish people only once a year, on the Day of Atonement (Leviticus 23:32). The Pharisees voluntarily fasted twice a week to impress the people with their 'holiness.' Jesus commended acts of self-sacrifice done quietly and sincerely. He wanted people to serve him for the right reasons, not from a selfish desire for praise" (*Life Application Bible,* Wheaton, IL: Tyndale, 1988, p. 1337).

Question 10. For a detailed look at God's view of our "fasting," see Isaiah 58.

STUDY 9: THE CHRISTIAN'S PRAYER

Question 2. Notice that Jesus did not tell them to pray in his own name because he had not yet explained his death and its significance to them. He did this later in John 14.

Question 4. The *name* stands for all God is—his being and nature, his character and attributes.

STUDY 10: THE CHRISTIAN'S TREASURE

Question 8. Some Bible versions use the word *mammon* for money. "Scholars disagree on the exact derivation of the word *mammon*. It is possible that it comes from a Hebrew word that means 'to trust' and that it was used to refer to whatever one places one's trust in for security. We do know that in Jesus' world the word *mammon* was used for property in general. It had a neutral meaning and was not considered to be something that was tainted with evil. It simply referred to wealth or anything of value. It is striking that when Jesus uses the term it always has a negative sense. For him mammon is hazardous material" (Dockery and Garland, *Seeking the Kingdom,* p. 92).

STUDY 11: THE CHRISTIAN'S DISCERNMENT

Question 8. "Dogs and pigs traditionally were considered unclean and unpleasant and held in low esteem (see Exodus 22:31; 2 Peter 2:22). The Jews employed both terms to describe heathen Gentiles (Matthew 15:26; Mark 7:27) and acted condescendingly toward them. With this background, it is most likely that Jesus is speaking of offering...the 'pearls' of the kingdom (the reference is primarily to the teaching of the kingdom) to unreceptive and hostile listeners" (Dockery and Garland, *Seeking the Kingdom,* p. 105, with reference to David Wenham, *The Parables of Jesus,* Downers Grove, IL: InterVarsity, 1989, pp. 174-75).

STUDY 12: THE CHRISTIAN'S EXPECTATION

Question 8. "Multiply that (Matthew 7:9-10) by infinity and that is God's attitude toward his child. In our folly we are apt to think that God is against us when something unpleasant happens to us. But God is our Father; and as our Father he will never give us anything that is evil" (Lloyd-Jones, *Studies in the Sermon on the Mount,* vol. 2, p. 203).

STUDY 13: THE CHRISTIAN'S DIRECTION

Question 4. "The narrow way may not be parallel to the broad way, but right in the middle of the broad stream of humanity. The difference is that all the traffic on it flows in the opposite direction" (Stanley Mooneyham, *Dancing on the Strait and Narrow: A Gentle Call to a Radical Faith,* New York: Harper & Row, 1989).

Question 5. We are warned about false prophets in both Old and New Testaments. Jeremiah spoke of them extensively in Jeremiah 23, and in Jeremiah 6:14 he said of them, "They dress the wound of my people as though it were not serious. 'Peace, peace,' they say, when there is no peace."

In 2 Peter 2:1-3 we read, "But there were also false prophets among the people, just as there will be false teachers among you. They will secretly introduce destructive heresies, even denying the sovereign Lord who bought them—bringing swift destruction on themselves. Many will follow their shameful ways and will bring the way of truth into disrepute. In their greed these teachers will exploit you with stories they have made up. Their condemnation has long been hanging over them, and their destruction has not been sleeping."

STUDY 14: THE CHRISTIAN'S RESPONSE

Question 2. "'On that day' points to a scene at the final judgment (cf. Joel 2:1; Amos 5:18; Malachi 3:17-18). False prophets will protest on that Day of Judgment that they proclaimed the kingdom message and did kingdom deeds, listing their credentials as driving out demons and working miracles (cf. Acts 19:13-16)" (Dockery and Garland, *Seeking the Kingdom,* p. 117).

Question 3. "Jesus never denies that false prophets could have performed 'miracles' or 'signs' (cf. Revelation 13:13-14). What he does deny is that he has or has had anything to do with them.... Our calling involves being discerning and alert. Yet we should note in this context (Matthew 7:15-23) that the ultimate verdict regarding the false teachers comes from the Judge, not the disciples" (Dockery and Garland, *Seeking the Kingdom,* pp. 117-18).

The Fisherman Bible Studyguide Series—
Get Hooked on Studying God's Word

Old Testament Studies

Genesis

Proverbs

New Testament Studies

Mark

John

Acts 1-12

Acts 13-28

Romans

Philippians

Colossians

James

1, 2, 3 John

Revelation

Women of the Word

Becoming Women
of Purpose

Wisdom for
Today's Woman

Women Like Us

Women Who
Believed God

For more information, visit our Web site: www.waterbrookmultnomah.com

Topical Studies

Building Your House on the Lord

Discipleship

Encouraging Others

The Fruit of the Spirit

Growing Through Life's Challenges

Guidance and God's Will

Higher Ground

Lifestyle Priorities

The Parables of Jesus

Parenting with Purpose and Grace

Prayer

Proverbs & Parables

The Sermon on the Mount

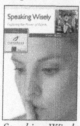
Speaking Wisely

Spiritual Disciplines

Spiritual Gifts

Spiritual Warfare

The Ten Commandments

When Faith Is All You Have

Who Is the Holy Spirit?